Song for My Left Ear, Song for My Right

poems by

Jim Richards

Finishing Line Press
Georgetown, Kentucky

Song for My Left Ear, Song for My Right

for Debbie

Copyright © 2025 by Jim Richards
ISBN 979-8-89990-084-6 First Edition
All rights reserved under International and Pan-American Copyright Conventions. No part of this book may be reproduced in any manner whatsoever without written permission from the publisher, except in the case of brief quotations embodied in critical articles and reviews.

Publisher: Leah Huete de Maines
Editor: Christen Kincaid
Cover Art: James Clayton
Author Photo: Jim Richards
Cover Design: Elizabeth Maines McCleavy

Order online: www.finishinglinepress.com
also available on amazon.com

Author inquiries and mail orders:
Finishing Line Press
PO Box 1626
Georgetown, Kentucky 40324
USA

Contents

I.

Childhood Is a Small Country 1
Petrology 3
Road Trip 4
A Black Spot 5
The Sting 6
Delay 7
The Cave 8
Horses for Hire 9
Kissing Boys 10
Little Ones 11
Chopping 12
Song for My Left Ear, Song for My Right 14
Obituary 15
Dressing the Corpse of My Grandfather 16
Bury Me Face Down 17

II.

The Beginning 21
Application 22
Working 23
Doctor 24
Some Minutes 25
On Days 26
Between Answer and Question 27
Your Mom 28
A Minor Planet 29
For Lack of Contrast 31
Remembering *Remembering Plato* 32
Exists Reason to Dance 33
Light Music 34
What We Look Forward To 35
An Early Education 36
The Tire Place 37

The Wheel 38
Bluetooth 40
Why Some People Are More Attractive Than Others 41
A Little Light 42
An Exercise in Scales 43
Her Music Plays 44
Who Is She? 45
Aphorisms 46

III.

Where I'm Headed 51
Impression-management Consultant 52
The Big League 53
Hotel Management 54
The Grave-filler's Instructions 55
I You and You Me 56
Top Secret 57
Meta Meta Etcetera 58
Let's 59
Pure Speculation 60
Some 61

I.

Childhood Is a Small Country

We were all born there
at one time or another and gazed
at the great mountains and tall trees.
When did we leave and why?

I remember a dirt road
with grass growing down the center
and small white flowers.
This highway is not the road.

I remember yellow hills
on the horizon, a grove of aspens,
the breeze. Where I am,
there are no hills.

Sometimes I sleep like a coin
falling to the ocean floor. In the morning,
I find myself in that country, in a quiet room,
and walk to the window to bathe in sunlight.

Even now, I remember that window,
how clean the glass was,
how paint peeled along the pane,
the motion of the curtain.

Sometimes the way to that place
is as simple as combing hair,
slicing cucumber, or looking for a shoe.
Sometimes I walk through a door

and find myself there
on the bank of the river—
how clean and how clear,
how fast it vanishes under the bridge.

The field where we played
within the call of our mother's voice.
The stars we slept under.
The island we had in a green lake,

the wild strawberries. We are all exiles,
trying to return, afraid of returning.
Do you remember the red fruit
and how our mouths ached with eating?

Petrology

A son isn't a story
to be told to strangers
for their pleasure.

A son is a conglomerate
rock with a swirl of color
and layers of pressure.

You cannot reach
into the womb of earth
and deliver this stone.

You cannot crack
the gem open to read
the crystallization of stars

mapping his universe.
You can only lie at night
on the floor beside his crib,

hold a finger out for him
to grasp until his crying
ends and yours begins.

Road Trip

Do you remember
as a child
coming home from a long road trip
half-asleep
but sensing the highway exit,
the stoplights,
the smell of the car, the turns telling you
where you are
without looking out the window?
The feeling
when you know you have pulled into
the driveway,
the door opens letting in a summer air
so familiar
all memory rushes back? You are home
and the arms
of someone strong enough to carry you
have lifted you,
and you could walk but you pretend
to be asleep
because your head is on the shoulder
of one who
cares enough to take you away for a while
and bring you back
to a place you didn't know
you loved.

A Black Spot

The first bird I shot
was a robin with my BB gun.
I was looking into the sun
at a tall pine where a black spot
flickered on a long limb.
I aimed and fired, not
expecting anything to happen,
but a winged shadow fell
to the forest floor. I ran
to see what I had hit
and found a punctured breast,
three beads of blood.
With two sticks, I picked up
the limp, feathered song,
help me forget, and flung it
into the woods.
I climbed the tall pine
and discovered—help me—a nest
of chicks, their orange beaks open,
trembling flames of fire.
I did not dirge *I killed your mother*
and cast myself to the ground.
No. I sang a single copper note
down each throat, ran
inside when called for supper.

The Sting

The farthest thing from fear
is a bee that lands on the finger
of a toddler who has never seen
a bee before. She smiles at it—
the transparent black wings,
the furry head, the black stripes
and, oh, the yellow as if the sun
bled itself there. No use rushing
to her to brush the bee away.
No use breaking the blessing
that has landed on her pointer
and is now walking to the back
of her hand. She will feel the sting
soon enough, and she will wail
pure, as if being born again.

Delay

Build a little hut
of sticks
to hold your heart in,
daughter,

in the dirt behind
the hangar.
Where is your father?
A little hole

to bury your socks in.
Is that
the world shaking or
the engine

of the crop duster?
A little dirt
beneath your fingernails
won't hurt.

An ocean
of sky above you. Do you
(you must)
believe in water?

The Cave

A child finds a cave in a cliff along the beach,
leaves the sun
and eases into darkness,
the air a cool shock.
                The sound of dripping water,
echo of surf.
                His eyes adjust, but soon he has to lift
his hands and feel his way. He caresses wet rock
and hand by hand
                follows it deeper into mystery,
each step a test.
                Only the cave knows how far a boy will go
before he turns and runs back to the sun, to the warm sand,
to the woman charging waist-deep
                through the breakers, searching for him,
shouting his name.

Horses for Hire

Horses are enough to make me worry about the world,
their necks thick and heavy, full of blood,
their bellies so big I want to be in them.
Their ears are enough—skin without bones—
the first time I touched one I could hear with my hand,
my arm, and into my shoulder blade.
Their manes make me violent in the heart, the hair
tangled and coated with dust—good dirty.
When veins rise on their long faces,
when their black eyeballs with heavy lids and lashes
look out at me with unnerving sadness,
when that sound climbs out of them
like a scream buried in gravel
and their round lips erupt with wet thunder,
when they raise their tails
and make shining orbs out of apples, oats, and grass,
when sweat streaks their sides in the sun,
when they smell like saddles—it is enough.
And when one walks to me, like this palomino,
its bridled head hung low as if it were ashamed
of making the boy on its back so happy, it's too much.

Kissing Boys

When was the last time I kissed him,
my eldest son, on the mouth?
I can't remember. When did I start
turning away and offering cheek
instead of lips? Somewhere between
our last kiss and today's awkwardness
we forgot the words to an old song.
How long before we turn not only cheeks
but backs to our affection, as I did
with my father? In the beginning,
my mouth was wet with infant kisses
from lips that couldn't speak, a tongue
that knew nothing but milk. Today,
I shake his hand. And near the end, love
will stand between us like slabs of stone.

Little Ones

Are these the words?
The ones that make milk keep?
The ones that say, *for you I care for words?*

Don't think of toys. Think balled, tired birds.
It's dark. Please go to sleep.
Are these the words?

The violent stare. The steady hand. Tin foil swords.
Small heart, which of these is deep?
The one that says, *for you I care for words.*

You are lucky. You are good. You walk toward a busy street.
These are the words.
Oh please. (Oh please, Oh please.) Beat.

I do. I care for you. I care for words.
Who should you believe? We walk in herds.
The pain in the nerves. The hands. The feet. These are the words.
The ones that say, *for you I care for words.*

Chopping

My hands are not trembling,
they are typing,
feeling the keyboard
as if it were hot.

Through the open window
I hear the maul
bursting through pine
and inhale the viscid scent of sap.

I sit inside and rhyme
while my father splits logs
as I've seen him split before—

at his age the ax hovers
above his head as though uncertain
before memory brings it down
and strikes a blow. I surely

disappointed him as a boy
when at camp with my hatchet
hacking away at a wet log
the blunt blade glance off and split
open the skin above my ankle,
touching bone. Lucky for me

my scoutmaster, an obstetrician,
knew how to deliver a boy
from error. With xylocaine
and a curved suture he laced
and tied my skin together,
cinching it like a shoe. But the cut

that occurred when my father heard
about my blunder is a wound
I am still trying to close. Good
and kind, he held me, as his father
once held him. We let each other down

from generation to generation.
I feel it each time he reads
these chopped up lines. The balance
of the ax as it swings up and behind,
the hands coming together, the stroke
that splits a dark shape open
to reveal its light—there is love

in this. But how can we praise
what we don't understand?
My fingers are not trembling,
they are typing,
feeling the keyboard
as if it were my father's wound.

Song for My Left Ear, Song for My Right

Still well asleep but waking warm in bed
with one ear muffled against the pillow,
my other catches music—a child playing
an upright piano, practicing a melody
that I played as a boy. My mind plinks
along a note ahead and feels a simple
joy each time he finds the key. Brief song,
but morning holds the damper pedal down

for years, until I turn my head to muffle
my left ear and expose the right, which hears
the same tune played by the same child
with ranges now that reach beyond the room.
The boy is gone. The father, well asleep
but waking, rocks side to side his ringing skull.

Obituary

He fell from fatherhood and said the fall
was slow, like water through wood.

He said he didn't know. That's all.
And then the undertow of life swept

his feet. The wash of salt and foam,
the steady crash brought things ashore:

his wallet, a little cash, a picture
of the dog. One shoe then the other

filled with seaweed. His body never rose.
His name? I don't know his name.

Call him you. Call him me. All I know
is that he fell, and he said the fall was slow.

Dressing the Corpse of My Grandfather

You died three days ago,
after one-hundred years. Your body
on this metal table is just as cold.

Three years ago, I bathed you,
dried you with nothing
but a towel between my hands and your skin.
I pulled socks over your ankles,
swollen like pears.

By then you could not hit my hand away
as you did years before
when I reached for the wool cap
you dropped on the lawn.

No. I handled you and your possessions.
I fed you fruit cocktail from a red dish
and wiped your lips with a paper napkin.

I fit your name between my names like a city,
the way you fit your father's between yours.

Now I force clothing over the aspen
of your arms and legs, so stiff
I might break you as you have broken me,
departure. Earlobe hard as stone.

When my father kissed your cold head,
Grandfather,
it felt like he was kissing me.

Bury Me Face Down

Back to the world,
eyes to the fiery core,
hand at the curtain of clay,
and ear to the door.

A slow journey, dark.
A gradual seeping, slow.
Not step by frozen step
but drip by drip I go.

No box to nail me in.
No balm to keep me fresh.
A faster, fetid form
to speed my running rest.

The looters will discover
if they disturb my land,
a vanished soul's impression,
a shadow made of sand.

II.

The Beginning

This is the beginning.
How many more legs
torn from their sockets
will be hung from the bridge?

The beginning is mud
warming in the sun
until what was soft is hard.
Five are hanging already.

There must be a beginning,
people say. And so an end.
But I believe these legs
have always been hanging

from this bridge, which has
always joined the roads
that web the earth, over a river
forever tainted with blood.

Application

We want your name.
Yes, we must have that.
No name? Paste the stamps
from your forehead onto the page.

We take what we can.
Numbers, we want them all.
This might hurt a bit.
When the tears come,
seal them in the tiny envelopes provided.

We will accept cotton pockets
in place of envelopes.
Your hands must be in them.

Stare at the third page till you see
yourself. Tear out your eyes
along the perforation.
Keep them for your records.

The buzzing you hear is normal.
The bells are not. Let the doctor push
his ring-finger between your ribs
to stop the swinging. Move carefully

for four months. Swallow
no ice. If you need to cough
use sign language, unless
you have sent us your hands.
In that case, we cannot help you.

Working

Don't bother me, I'm working.
It may appear that I'm asleep,
sprawled out, facedown
on the bed, but I am working.

*

Leave me alone, so I can concentrate.
You may think I lie lazily
in this hammock, but I assure you
I am focused, hence my closed eyes.

*

Please, go away. I cannot stare
so vacantly into the void
when you are around. And by stare
vacantly into the void, I mean working.

*

Working, working, working,
and never paid a cent. The hardest labor
is yet to come: when I am dead,
lying in my grave. Do not disturb me.

Doctor

When you check me, look deep.
I lost something in all that darkness.
When you examine my ears,
fine-tune the small bones for music.
I want to hear tree trunks chant
and the open sky belt its blues.
I want the croon of muddy rivers.
And when you take my blood,
replace it with an injection of moonlight,
enough to make me glow for a while
like a field of snow on a clear night.

Some Minutes

Each minute is an oval
to be filled in on a test,

a small hole in the lawn
a skunk dug looking for grubs.

How many minutes fly
like a flock of trash bags?

Once I found the roadside
remains of a mule deer buck—

when I clutched an antler
and lifted its head, minutes

squirmed in a pile, fat with flesh.
I cut off the head and took it home.

The bag of marbles I had as a child
was full of minutes I could hold

between thumb and finger and launch
at another glass ball of time.

Now the universe moves so slowly
I can hardly advance without bumping

into stalled stars. Each winter I unscrew
the hose from the spigot,

shake out the last few minutes
and hang it over the deck to drip.

Something must be done with time
before it freezes and bursts the line.

On Days

They come one after another, so be prepared.
No, there is no end to them. Even if you end,
the days go on and on.

They come with different weather, so be prepared.
Yes, there will be cold and rain. Even when you're cold,
the days go on and on.

They come filled with seconds, minutes, hours,
so be prepared. It is difficult
to spend them all, yet there are never enough.

You cannot be prepared for some days—
I should have made that clear. Certain days,
the worst ones, will pierce you. Those days,

you will live over and over. This is all
that is known about days, so be prepared. This,
and the fact that some days are warm.

But you cannot prepare for warm days.
You can only let them hold you when they arrive
and try to recall them when they are gone.

Between Answer and Question

I can't tell
the difference

between a song
and a scream,

a backslash
and a slash back.

Can you teach me?
I can't feel

the difference
between an ocean

of hope and
a lake of despair,

a sinking
and a surfacing.

Can you reach me?
My hand is open

but my heart is closed,
your heart is open

but you grip a gun.
I can't tell the difference

between answer and
question. Is there one?

Your Mom

Psst. What's your mom like?
Abe Lincoln called his mom an angel. Would you
call yours an angel? Does she ever call you *my angel*?
Does she believe in angels?
Can she cut hair? Can she cook?
Does she consider herself a career woman?
Is she a dog person? Seems like everyone is a dog person these days.
How many children did she have? Is she divorced?
Would you say you know everything about her?
Or is she the type you don't know anything about?
If a mirror is on the floor, will she look down at it?
Would she walk on it? What does she weigh?
Does she retain water? Is she an expert at anything?
Do fellas gawk at her and follow her around?
Can she field a grounder? When it comes to the fiddle,
how's her fingering? How's about a little help here?
I'm doing my best, aren't I? JK. LOL.
My mom and your mom are friends, aren't they?
No, I said friends not sisters. I mean we're not cousins, right?
But I'm open to that. At least I'm not opposed to it.
I guess we'd have to look into our genealogy.
There's a missionary who can help us with that.
Maybe our parents' parents' parents were polygamists.
Well, it's possible, isn't it? The queen's parents were.
Quick, hide, someone's coming.

A Minor Planet

A minor planet is named after him. That's all I know.
Does he like mustard on his dog?
I don't know. I only know that a planet is named after him.
What is the first thing he does in the morning?
What kind of music does he like?
No clue. Beyond the planet naming, I know nothing.
Does he buy and sell on Craigslist?
Are his initials written or embroidered on any of his clothing?
What does he think of Švankmajer's films?
Does he use hot sauce?
How many sit-ups could he do in his prime?
Are his feet exactly the same size?
I'm telling you, I don't know anything about him, besides the planet thing.
Does he dirge on occasion?
What cupboard did he hide in as a boy?
Was he ever a bumblebee killer?
What was he yelling about when he was supposed to be yodeling?
How long has it been since he went to the zoo?
Is he more for Plato or Archimedes?
Could a cloud be said to have passed through him?
Does he dog-ear borrowed books?
Has he ever seen a severe case of elephantiasis firsthand?
Is he apt to help fill the firefighter's boot?
Grocery bags—paper? plastic? brings his own?
How hot is his iron at its hottest?
In any instance, has his irritability made him irate?
What are his thoughts on Jews for Jesus?
How does he feel about marketing misspells, like Krispy Kreme?
I won't ask about emojis, but is he into acronyms like *lol*?
How sad has he been, and does it show?
Would people be surprised, say, if he became a mass shooter?
Can you at least tell me his name and number?
Would he know about omphaloskepsis or turophilia?
Is he opposed to pineapple on pizza?
Has he ever rolled his own quarters?
Is he rich?
Does he play squash or eat it?
When he takes the train, how does he occupy his fancy?

Does he ever carry an umbrella?
If he's not a vegetarian or vegan, what's his view on venison?
Wow. Just wow.
Can he waterski? If so, can he cross the wake?
Does he have an ex?
Look, a minor planet is named after him. That's all I know.
Then what is the name of the planet?
It's the same as his name. Maybe you can tell me.

For Lack of Contrast

On the black wall, someone
has painted a black dog.

On the green wall, a green cat.
You get the picture.

Yet I go on. In the invisible sky,
an invisible airplane.

What is the handless man
holding in his hands?

The heart of a heartless lover.
What song was the woman singing

when she lost her voice, her mouth
open like the cone

of a sleeping volcano, now filled
with a depthless lake?

Come to me, little field mouse,
whisper the answer in the place

where I once had an ear.
Or was it an eye?

Remembering *Remembering Plato* (Installation by Mineko Grimmer)

Forget that you have come to a museum,
to a cave. Forget
that two inverted, frozen cones of ice and gravel
are suspended from
the ceiling, melting in a spotlight, disintegrating
and falling into
separate pools of water. Forget the light, the shadows
on the wall. Forget
the single wire stretched across a pool, beneath a cone,
a bar across a pool,
beneath a cone; is there a mirror here, are you a mirror,
am I? Forget the notes
that ring when ice decides at last that it is water
and gravel falls.
Ringing of a string, clink-call of a bar, echo in a cave,
forget it all.
Through your senses you have abandoned sense,
become a drop
of water hanging on a stone, both of you about
to fall and make
two notes of music, about to translate gravity
into sound, and sound
into waves of water, and water into light, and shadows
into shadows.

Exists Reason to Dance

Translation fails. But body
knows exists reason to shake it
with your eyes clenched shut
head looping, arms flailing
as though shark had leg of you
and held you lovingly under water.
Exists logic for hips to quicken
as a coin piece stopping spinning.
For hips to thrust hard and hard
against the invisible. Warrant
to roll from heel to toe, to turn
and kick and hop. Be a question
mark spinning round. Be a solo.

Light Music

Return, and let the floodlight fill you
as the sun's silence fills the morning train.
If you stay in darkness, it can kill you.

Consider the seed that waits beneath the soil,
still until the warming weather calls:
return, and let the sunlight fill you.

A song swirls unwritten in the void
until the writer whispers: *come out,*
if you stay in silence, it will kill you.

Then the music plays and, as a star
that sends its light into infinity, the waves
return and like a floodlight fill you.

The future is a lamp, the past is singing
in a circle, an ancient hymn that says:
if you pray, the darkness cannot kill you.

Consider what your sacred texts reveal:
body is bell, breath the morning peal.
Return, and let the ringing thrill you.
If you become the music, light can heal you.

What We Look Forward To

Wasn't tomorrow nice,
the way it hovered before us
like a helium balloon unable to rise
for the weight of its string but not

sinking either? Tomorrow was a room
empty but ready for guests with tables full of food
and drink, cushioned chairs arranged, dim light,
music coming from nowhere. It was

a singular event anticipated, a child
standing on a runway, looking up at
the rising jets, an empty picture frame
given as a gift. Honestly, it was you—

your vague face, your voice, your scent
after a shower. Tomorrow was all of this,
but terrible we had to turn around.
What we look forward to now is yesterday.

An Early Education

Today, class, we are going to learn
how to use tally marks
in case you are ever imprisoned
and need to measure your days,
dripping like water in a cell.

You will need chalk or stone.
You will need a wall (or walls,
depending on the length of your sentence).
When you have made four lines,
slash across them with the fifth, like

this. Right to left, top to bottom.
If you have no chalk or stone,
use blood. Don't giggle, children,
pay attention. This may save you
a lot of time counting and recounting.

The Tire Place

In the waiting room
the smell of tires, stale popcorn,
and spilled Mellow Yellow.

The sounds of WWE
on the television, torque guns
in the shop zapping lug nuts.

A child is throwing a tantrum
because his mother
won't let him lick the floor.

Out in the world a virus
is spreading, people deciding how
and when to panic. Stocks

plunge and surge. A screw
has punctured my all-weather tire,
and they are fixing it for free.

An advertisement for ED
on the television seems
to calm the child. I'm listening

to *Macbeth* on audiobook—
"Remember the porter."
A technician with greasy hands

drops my keys on the counter and asks
if I have any questions. Just one—
I write it down and slide it to him.

The Wheel

It was supposed to be a child
but it was a wheel
that was born. The midwife
was startled
and didn't know whether to spank it
or not. She decided simply
to clean it, dry it off, and hand it
to the mother.

The mother refused
to acknowledge anything abnormal.
She loved it, kissed it, held it to her breast.
There was no father.

Easy to care for,
the wheel needed no cradle,
no rocking to sleep, no nursing,
but the mother did all these with pleasure
because she loved the wheel like her own flesh.

She taught it to roll. She taught it to spin.
She took it to the park
where the other children played with it
or abandoned it if they became bored.

Once a boy struck it with a stick
for no apparent reason. The mother pushed him
away and took her wheel up into her arms.
She sang to it, read it stories, and one might say
it was the happiest wheel that had ever been born.

The mother loved her wheel lifelong
and, when she grew old, she died with the wheel
by her side. The wheel was discarded
with her knickknacks by fools who didn't know better.
But the wheel dreamed of rolling beyond this life
someday and reuniting with its mother.

There it is, in the corner of the thrift store
leaning against the wall. No one has touched it
for years, and it longs for the warmth of flesh.
No one imagines it has a memory and a soul
as tender as any human's. No one knows the wheel
can feel, and that is the most painful loneliness of all.

Bluetooth

It was Gutenberg, back for a visit.
I took him to Chipotle, then, in the park,
we climbed trees. Huge oaks. Near
the top of one, where the branches

were weaker and yielding to our weight,
he confessed: I do not believe in miracles
anymore. Then I have something
to show you, I said. We walked

to my office on campus, I typed
a few words on my laptop, then printed them
via Bluetooth. I thought it would
amaze him. I thought he would bow down

and worship me. I already told you,
he said, I do not believe in miracles anymore.

Why Some People Are More Attractive Than Others

It's been a hard day for technology.
A laptop slid off the desk onto a tile floor.
A cell phone fell into a bowl of minestrone.
Poor tech! So broken and neglected.
An Xbox was smashed with the back
of an ax. A smartwatch was slammed
in the door of a Prius. How can technology
survive all of this violence? Pity tech.
A butterfly is hovering over a pile
of ergonomic keyboards at the landfill.
Woe! Woe! Woe! Woe! Woe! Woe!

A Little Light

> *God, do not judge! You were never a woman on this earth.*
> —Marina Tsvetaeva

The horrors are beginning to be known
and should continue to evaporate from the saturated earth
until they fill the sky and fill our lungs,
and may we never stop breathing them ages without end
lest we forget and choke on pure air.

In the meantime, at least at this moment,
a little light. A single match offering flame for a few seconds
in a dismal cave. A lamp beside an old armchair
in which one reads and weeps. Or dare I say a single star
in a night sky full of dark clouds above the city?

Here: a table set for two. Only one is there,
but the food is ready. A carrot chutney with cumin, spread
on warm bread. A buckwheat and red pepper
salad in vinaigrette. A dish of sliced peaches and sweet potatoes
with arugula and fresh cream cheese.

These are not mere pleasures. Pleasure
is fleeting. These are memories, ingested like fruit, becoming
part of the sweetness of the body forever.
And when that body is planted again in the earth, as all are,
the sweetness rises to garnish the horrors.

An Exercise in Scales

Light loves you, woman,
this morning, makes your
shape move like sheets in
wind. Come to me as
clay to wet hands, as
blue crows to the crushed
snake on the roadside.

*

Light loves you, woman.
This is the oath I've
shaped my life to, as
wind shapes stone, water
clay. At you, the bold
blue skies blush, and the
snakes all shed their skin.

*

Light loved you! Why then
this grave and stone? Your
shape disintegrates as
wind strolls over the
clay that cradles your
blue skin. My heart: a ball of
snakes floating in a flood.

*

Light is longer than
this time we call love,
shape more solid than
a woman made of wind.
When the clay dries, breaks,
a new form grows a tongue.
Words swallow the worms.

Her Music Plays

Up north I know a field of grass
Wealthy with her yawns.
When worms curl and turn their thoughts
She buries them in songs.

She lives on bones of hollow birds
On cattle-tears and pies.
Her herbs are clover, sage; her salt
Mosquitoes, pepper flies.

She taught me mow and trim and tear,
I taught her where and when.
More striking than the wildest flower,
Her shadow leaves a stain.

Her talk is all tautologies,
She argues with the moon.
The proofs that she can generate
Are blades, silvery, new.

Rarely is she moved, except
By wind and badger breast.
So sweet is fur and field's exchange,
The clouds begin to sweat

And heaven's farmers drop their eyes
To watch her take the rain.
Fresh from the morning shower she shines,
Her skins all cold and clean.

She's sharp, ears up, with echoes on,
A buzzing in her drums.
And if not ears then flames of mint,
And if not flames then tongues.

Who and what and why am I
Is every sound she sings.
Her music shakes my bones all day,
She makes my marrow green.

Who Is She?

Who dies for truth? Whose hands
and wrists are tied behind the pole,
flames rising at her feet?
Who looks down and sees her toes
hanging off the edge of the plank,
the raw ocean surging below?
Who catches a glimpse of her face
in the reflection of the guillotine?
Who sings before the firing squad, her voice
so strong one soldier aims to miss?
Who bares her breast to the bayonet?
Who kneels and looks heavenward
as stones fly at her from all sides?
Who is the woman on the cross with blood
dripping from the ends of her hair?

Aphorisms

Rare birds are surprised
to see people.

*

The key won't fit because this is not my car.
Or these are not my keys. Or both.

*

This idea preoccupied the Roman stoics:
don't be preoccupied with death.

*

She was born in March. They named her June.
You do the math.

*

From darkness one must close one's eyes
to enter great light.

*

The sky remains the same whether I praise or blame it.
Yet the sky is always changing.

*

Where I'm going doesn't appear on the highway sign.
But there is an exit.

*

My thoughts are strangers,
but I entertain them constantly.

*

I wonder who will stop
and move that rock in the road.

*

The more I need to go to bed
the harder it is to get there.

*

A kiss is just a kiss.
Unless it's the kiss of death.

III.

Where I'm Headed

I'm going the other direction via the Road of Imbeciles to the Village of Idiots. The wise and well-informed are too predictable. In their town, you cannot find someone with a parsnip in his pocket, or a lady singing through a hole in her top hat. Try such nonsense on their turf and they'll banish you forthwith. (Psst, don't say *forthwith*—they have a growing list of unacceptable terms.) But in Schmucksville, you can say whatever you want and no one's earlobes burn. Even the wise and well-informed are welcome, but they don't stick around for long.

Impression-management Consultant

A homeless man wearing a black overcoat, standing before a shop window, looks though his reflection to a leather jacket hanging on a headless mannequin. A rat peeks at him from the gutter grate, watching for crumbs to fall from bread the man keeps in his holey pockets. The man and the rat are on intimate terms since they share this corner of sidewalk. Between them rushes a stream of people, each with a phone in hand, except for one young woman who is carrying a book. As the rain comes on, the people rush faster, and the sound of their shoes on wet concrete increases the city's treble. The rain comes harder, so the rat ducks into his crack, the homeless man wanders off, and the woman, who is wearing heels, hurries down the sidewalk holding the book above her head.

The Big League

When Emily Dickinson wandered onto the baseball field mid-game, play stopped, but no one chased her as they might chase a streaking fan—perhaps because she wasn't running or wasn't naked. Her angle took her past first base toward center field and her gaze was fixed on something far away. *She wants to pick that dandelion,* shouted a know-it-all who cheered for the other team. But there were no dandelions in the freshly mown field. *Shut it you nimrod,* came the reply. A fight ensued, and things were seen that are rarely seen without a fight: a chili dog entered a falling man's armpit; a t-shirt was stretched to the length of a skirt; a bead from a broken necklace landed in a cup of beer. Emily slowly made her way to the other side as people were distracted with more pressing spectacles, but in her wake she left a strange and memorable violence, a slap of the mind followed by a slant echo in the heart. Soon enough the fools were escorted out of the stadium, and the long and boring game resumed.

Hotel Management

When I stopped worrying about beauty so many possibilities appeared. I wrapped a plastic knife, spoon, and fork in a paper napkin, and sealed it in plastic. I didn't need to explain it anymore. I was content to wipe my feet on a worn-out welcome mat. I stopped charging my tenants for leaving their mirrors on at night. If I needed art, I could hang a rag on the wall and frame it. (Please clean your hair out of the sink.) But beauty is different from confusion—it tries to creep back in. I look over my shoulder when I'm sitting at the front desk and see myself looking over my shoulder. (This uniform has a stain, that one doesn't.) I need to hire someone new for the night shift. Are you interested?

The Grave-filler's Instructions

Your job isn't to dig the hole it's to fill the hole, see,
with that pile over there, and this is your shovel, okay,
and once the king is in there then you scoop a shovelful
and throw it in on top of the king, and then you put
the queen in because the lady is always on top
and—I don't know why that's just the way it is the lady
is always on top—and then you take another shovelful
and you throw it in, and you start with a shovelful
of this, and then the heavier stuff that smells like mice
and then the children come and they cry and they leave
and then you plant grass on it and you have to water
the grass, don't forget to water the grass. Now get going.

I You and You Me

The problem with understanding is that it never happens. A spouse, a lover, a friend says, *I understand you,* but they don't. A pet stares at you with that look but has no clue. The soldier on her back, a boot on her chest, a barrel between her lips thinks she gets it, and so does the guy on the other end of the gun. I have seen two ants approach each other on the sidewalk and gesture with antennae for several minutes then scurry off in frustration. A goldfinch stood on my deck for an hour staring at the small crescent of feathers stuck to the window it had collided with, contemplating glass? gravity? *It was stunned*, you say, and I would agree. I went out to explain, but the bird kept putting its tail toward me. You understand, right? You know what I mean when I say understanding never happens? That's what I'm afraid of, this certainty we have when we stand under the stars and say we understand—I you and you me.

Top Secret

Carry around an envelope clearly stamped TOP SECRET. Be sure it is well sealed. Carry it outside of your briefcase or bag so all can see it. Place it on your desk where others will notice, and the cleaning crew will wonder. Keep it under your pillow some nights. Shuffle it among your mail. Let it appear accidentally in the background of photos. If anyone ever asks, simply say, *It's top secret*. Take it with you to dinner and set it next to your plate. It must be ready to be delivered at any moment in case the recipient arrives, cracking his enormous knuckles.

Meta Meta Etcetera

In the bedroom, a nightmare of a nightmare in which a poet poised before a typewriter writes an ekphrastic of MacLeish's "Ars Poetica."

In the basement, a pair of directors discuss the dos and don'ts of recording a director's commentary while watching the director's commentary on *Inception*.

Across the street, through the doors, down the hall, in the office, a teacher meets with a student to discuss her rhetorical analysis of Orwell's "Politics and the English Language."

Somewhere, John Malkovich is being the John Malkovich from *Being John Malkovich*.

Kids have snuck into the school library to watch: kids watching videos of kids playing video games; kids watching videos of kids watching music videos; kids watching videos of kids watching reaction videos.

Two of them will graduate from a program in which, at least once, they workshop a poem about workshopping a poem. One of them will become, at some point, a university administrator after taking classes on university administration.

For reasons that are unclear, the administrator will oppose the production of *The Murder of Gonzago* within the tragedy of *Hamlet* within *Rosencrantz and Guildenstern are Dead* as discussed during the talkback—a play about this.

All because of, perhaps: the mother inside the mother inside the mother, etc. At some level, we never wake up.

Let's

Let's let the ants have a little more time to dig their tunnels before we exterminate them. Let's see if the rope swing we tied in the pear tree has become an inextricable part of the branch. Let's not talk to the birds anymore. Let's calculate how many mittens have washed down the gutter into the sewer each spring, and then we'll consider scarves. I don't know who held this dollar bill before me, but it could have been a hacker. Let's go digital and deal with the drawbacks. Let's be sure to ask our guests, *How do you like your eggs?* Let's remember to listen. *Shall we wander into the shade?* Let's.

Pure Speculation

Relief from suffering might be finding its way across an ocean on a raft with a makeshift sail. Or perhaps a rogue tendril of joy will be discovered breaking through the soil beside a sprig of wild peppermint. Likewise, that tingling between your ribs is possibly pain growing an arm to drag itself away. And when the night clears, maybe grief will sleep alone under the stars, and wolves will devour it. All in all, if a fleet of hope finally arrives, the captain should not be surprised when we hold them at bay and say: *explain.*

Some

Some light is yellow as pinewood.
Some white, coming out of snow.
Some snow is black, after a long city-winter, blistered
by the wind. Some wind is warm,
but winter keeps it locked in a stone box.
When it seeps through the cracks, they say "spring."
When you hear it howl, it's imprisoned again.
Some prisons are good, like the prison of clothes—colors and fabrics
guarding what could hurt us most. Some women can hurt.
They can hurt for their whole lives. Some can escape
through that hole, sometimes, seep
their way out, like a sentence through the mouth saying:
Some world we live in.
Some heaven some say will come somehow.
Some ending to what we've survived for some time now.

ACKNOWLEDGMENTS

Grateful acknowledgment is made to the editors of the magazines and journals in which the following poems first appeared:

Alexandria Quarterly:	"Let's"
Clackamas Literary Review:	"I You and You Me" and "What We Look Forward To"
Copper Nickel:	"The Big League" and "Hotel Management"
Crack the Spine:	"Application" (Nominated for the Pushcart Prize)
Cumberland River Review:	"An Exercise in Scales"
Dreamers:	"Obituary"
Freshwater:	"Horses for Hire" (Nominated for the Pushcart Prize)
Hotel Amerika:	"Aphorisms"
International Poetry Review:	"Dressing the Corpse of My Grandfather"
Latitudes:	"Her Music Plays"
Literary Juice:	"Exists Reason to Dance"
Marathon Literary Review:	"Petrology"
Mud Season Review:	"Kissing Boys" and "Doctor"
North Dakota Quarterly:	"Light Music" and "On Days"
Poet Lore:	"Childhood Is a Small Country"
Poetry Northwest:	"Song for My Left Ear, Song for My Right"
Prairie Schooner:	"A Black Spot"
Relief:	"Pure Speculation"
Salt Hill:	"Why Some People Are More Attractive Than Others"
South Carolina Review:	"Delay"
Southern Poetry Review:	"The Cave"
Sugar House Review:	"Some Minutes" and "Bluetooth"
Treehouse:	"Impression-management Consultant"
Twisted Vine:	"Bury Me Face Down"
Verdad:	"Little Ones" and *"Remembering Remembering Plato"*

I am grateful to Lance Larsen, Susan Elizabeth Howe, Leslie Norris, Edward Hirsch, Adam Zagajewski, Marie Howe, and Mark Doty for their vital instruction and influence; to Jason Koo and Doug Talley for friendship and many defining conversations; to Bethany Schultz Hurst for reading and supporting; to the University of Houston and the Idaho Commission on the Arts for their generous fellowships; to James Clayton for the excellent cover art; to my friends and colleagues for their encouragement and comradery; to my mother and father for giving me life and language; to my five sons for bringing me joy; to Isaac for reading so carefully; and most of all to Debbie for so much love.

Jim Richards received a PhD in literature and creative writing from the University of Houston. His work has been nominated for *Best New Poets* and the Pushcart Prize. He was granted a Literary Arts Fellowship through the Idaho Commission on the Arts. He lives in Rexburg with his family and teaches at Brigham Young University-Idaho. This is his first collection of poetry.

www.ingramcontent.com/pod-product-compliance
Lightning Source LLC
Chambersburg PA
CBHW030058170426
43197CB00010B/1571